Pebble® Plus

PEOPLE OF THE U.S. ARMED FORCES
SAILORS
OF THE U.S. NAVY

by Jennifer Reed

Consulting Editor: Gail Saunders-Smith, PhD

Capstone press®

Mankato, Minnesota

Pebble Plus is published by Capstone Press,
151 Good Counsel Drive, P.O. Box 669, Mankato, Minnesota 56002.
www.capstonepub.com

022010
005713R

Library of Congress Cataloging-in-Publication Data
Reed, Jennifer, 1967 –
    Sailors of the U.S. Navy / by Jennifer Reed.
    p. cm. — (Pebble plus. People of the U.S. Armed Forces)
    Includes bibliographical references and index.
    Summary: "A brief introduction to a sailor's life in the Navy, including training, jobs, and life after
service" — Provided by publisher.
    ISBN-13: 978-1-4296-2251-6 (hbk.)
    ISBN-10: 1-4296-2251-2 (hbk.)
    1. United States. Navy — Juvenile literature. 2. Sailors — United States — Juvenile literature. I. Title.
VA58.4.R438 2009
359.3'30973 — dc22   2008026971

Editorial Credits
Gillia Olson, editor; Renée T. Doyle, designer; Jo Miller, photo researcher

Photo Credits
Capstone Press/Karon Dubke, 1, 21
Defense Imagery, 5
Shutterstock/RCPPHOTO, 22–23
U.S. Navy Photo by Jeff Doty, 17; by MC2 Nathan Laird, 10; by MC3 Ann Marie Lazarek, 11; by MC3 Kyle Gahlau,
    15; by MC3 Richard Waite, 19; by MCSN Kyle D. Gahlau, cover; by Mr. Scott A. Thornbloom, 7; by PH3 Kitt
    Amaritnant, 13; by PHC Eric A. Clement, 9

Artistic Effects
iStockphoto/walrusmail (rivets), cover, 1
Shutterstock/Jitloac (rope), 2–3, 24

Capstone Press thanks Dr. Sarandis Papadopoulos, Naval Historian, for his assistance with this book.

Note to Parents and Teachers

The People of the U.S. Armed Forces series supports national science standards related to
science, technology, and society. This book describes and illustrates sailors of the U.S. Navy.
The images support early readers in understanding the text. The repetition of words and
phrases helps early readers learn new words. This book also introduces early readers to
subject-specific vocabulary words, which are defined in the Glossary section. Early readers
may need assistance to read some words and to use the Table of Contents, Glossary, Read
More, Internet Sites, and Index sections of the book.

Table of Contents

Joining the Navy

Men and women join
the United States Navy
to protect the country.
They guard oceans and
waterways around the world.

Recruits have basic training

for eight weeks.

They exercise and

learn about ships.

They learn to fight fires.

Job Training

After basic training,

recruits become sailors.

Next, they train for their jobs.

Helmsmen steer ships.

Gunner's mates work
with missiles and guns.
They also take care
of the equipment
that fires these weapons.

Navy pilots fly
F/A-18 Hornets.
Directors guide pilots and
planes on the decks
of aircraft carriers.

F/A-18 Hornet

Director

13

Living in the Navy

Navy sailors see the world.

Many live on ships

for six months at a time.

Aircraft carriers

can hold 5,500 sailors.

Sailors who are not at sea

live and work

on naval bases.

Bases have stores, homes,

and hospitals.

Serving the Country

Most sailors serve

for four years.

Some sailors stay in the Navy

for 20 years or more.

After serving four years,

sailors may leave the Navy.

Some go to college.

Others use their training

and skills in civilian jobs.

Glossary

aircraft carrier — a warship with a large flat deck where aircraft take off and land

base — an area run by the military where people serving in the military live and military supplies are stored

basic training — the first training period for people who join the military; basic training is sometimes called boot camp.

civilian — not connected to the military; also, a person who is not in the military.

missile — a weapon that is fired at a target to blow it up

recruit — a person who has just joined the military

Read More

Garnett, Sammie, Jerry Pallotta, and Rob Bolster. *U.S. Navy Alphabet Book.* Watertown, Mass.: Charlesbridge, 2004.

Reed, Jennifer. *The U.S. Navy.* Military Branches. Mankato, Minn.: Capstone Press, 2009.

Internet Sites

FactHound offers a safe, fun way to find educator-approved Internet sites related to this book.

Here's what you do:

1. Visit *www.facthound.com*
2. Choose your grade level.
3. Begin your search.

This book's ID number is 9781429622516.

FactHound will fetch the best sites for you!

Index

Word Count: 165
Grade: 1
Early-Intervention Level: 22